MW01140382

Basic PRINCIPLES FOR THE SERVICE in the CHURCH LIFE

WITNESS LEE

Living Stream Ministry
Anaheim, California

First Edition, March 1999.

ISBN 0-7363-0608-0

Published by

Living Stream Ministry
2431 W. La Palma Ave., Anaheim, CA 92801 U.S.A.
P. O. Box 2121, Anaheim, CA 92814 U.S.A.

Printed in the United States of America

99 00 01 02 03 04 / 9 8 7 6 5 4 3 2 1

CONTENTS

PREFACE

This book is composed of messages given by Brother Witness Lee in a training in Altadena, California in the summer of 1963. Chapters one through three were previously published in *To Serve in the Human Spirit*. The remainder of the messages were not reviewed by the speaker.

CHAPTER ONE

THE SERVICE OF THE PRIESTHOOD

Scripture Reading: 1 Pet. 2:5, 9; Rom. 12:1-2, 4-7

In the Christian life there are always two aspects, the matter of life and the matter of service. As the Lord's children, we need a proper spiritual life, and we need the proper spiritual service. The proper Christian service is a matter of life, and it is in the Body. Such a spiritual service is presented as the priesthood in 1 Peter 2:5: "You yourselves also, as living stones, are being built up as a spiritual house into a holy priesthood to offer up spiritual sacrifices acceptable to God through Jesus Christ."

The holy priesthood in this verse is the spiritual house. The spiritual house built up together with the saints is the holy priesthood. The house is the priesthood, and the priesthood is the house. These are two aspects of one thing, two aspects of the building up together of the saints. This building up is the house of God, and it is the priesthood of God—not merely priests, but a priesthood.

Verse 9 continues with the royal priesthood: "But you are a chosen race, a royal priesthood, a holy nation, a people acquired for a possession, so that you may tell out the virtues of Him who has called you out of darkness into His marvelous light." This royal priesthood is the spiritual house. These three matters are crucial: the spiritual house, the holy priesthood, and the royal priesthood. On one hand, the priesthood is holy; on the other hand, the priesthood is royal.

Paul deals with the matter of the Christian life and the matter of the Christian service in the book of Romans. The service is in Romans 12: "I exhort you therefore, brothers, through the compassions of God to present your bodies a living sacrifice, holy, well pleasing to God, which is your reasonable service. And do not be fashioned according to this age, but be transformed by the renewing of the mind that you may prove what the will of God is, that which is good and well pleasing and perfect" (vv. 1-2). Many bodies are offered as one unique sacrifice, not many sacrifices, but one sacrifice with many bodies.

This good, acceptable, and perfect will of God is continued in verses 4-7: "For just as in one body we have many members, and all the members do not have the same function, so we who are many are one body in Christ, and individually members one of another. And having gifts that differ according to the grace given to us, whether prophecy, let us prophesy according to the proportion of faith; or service, let us be faithful in that service; or he who teaches, in that teaching." All the Christian services are in the Body. If you have the Body with the Body practice, the Body expression, and the Body life, then you have the Christian service.

LIFE AND SERVICE

In this chapter we are dealing with the practical aspect of the Christian life, that is, the service. With us as Christians there are always two aspects. The first aspect is a matter of the Christian life, a life matter, and the second aspect is a matter of the Christian service, a service matter. As the Lord's children, on the one hand we need a proper life, a spiritual life, and on the other hand we need a proper service, a spiritual service.

In Matthew 25 the Lord Jesus gave two parables, the parable of the ten virgins, which deals with the Christian life, and the parable of the talents, which is related to our service. As far as our life is concerned, we should be as the virgins with the testimony of light in our hand as we go out of this world to meet our Bridegroom. This is our life, the life aspect. We need the oil, and we need the testimony of light. We need to go out of this world, to wait for the Lord's coming back, and to go on to meet His coming. This is the Christian life.

Immediately following this parable, the Lord gave us the parable of the talents, which is something related to our service. We need to use the talent, the gift, which the Lord has given us, to do some business and to make some profit for the Lord. With the Lord's children there are always these two aspects, the life and the service. We need to grow in life with the oil, with the light, and with the going out of this world to meet the Lord in His coming back. We also need to exercise in a proper way what the Lord has given us as a gift, as a talent.

In the Epistle to the Romans the apostle Paul covers these two aspects. In the greater part of this book, the apostle deals with the aspect of life. Romans gives the sequence of the Christian walk, the Christian life. At the very beginning, in the first two and a half chapters, there is a sinner before God. Then in chapters three, four, and the first part of chapter five, this sinner is justified, forgiven, redeemed, and saved through the redemption of Christ. In the second part of chapter five through chapter eight, this redeemed, justified, and forgiven person is walking in the new life, in the Spirit. He realizes the fact that the old man has been put to death and the fact that with the old man there is nothing good. The old man, the old nature, has been put on the cross. Now the Spirit of Christ, as the embodiment of Christ as life to us, is living within us. We must walk according to Him and walk in Him. So this very one who was originally a sinner is now a saint, walking according to the Spirit. Then in chapter twelve so many redeemed ones who are walking in the Spirit are composed together in the Spirit as one Body. They are members of this one Body.

THE GROWTH IN LIFE

First we have the aspect of life, then the aspect of service. We have the life matter settled first, then, based on that fact, we have the matter of service. Without life and the adequate growth in life, we cannot have the service. The little children can do many things, but they cannot serve, because they simply do not have the adequate growth in life.

To serve the Lord, the growth in life is required. The service is not mentioned in Romans 6 or 7. It is not mentioned until chapter twelve, where sinners have been redeemed, justified, and delivered from the old nature, and they are walking in the Spirit. They have the real growth in life. Now they are the practical and functioning members of the Body. The Christian service is an issue of the growth of life.

If you do not have life, you cannot serve. Even if you have life but are short of the growth in life, still young, childish, and even like a babe, you cannot serve. The service requires life and the growth of life, the maturity of life. It is a life matter, and it is a matter of the growth in life. We cannot serve the Lord without growing in the life of the Lord. This is something very basic. This is why we have been stressing the matter of life in view of our expectation of having a church life with the service. Without the growth in life, there is no possibility for the church to be built up, and without the building up of the church, there is no possibility of having the church service, the Christian service.

SERVICE IN THE BODY

The Christian service is a matter of life and in the Body. It is a matter in the Body and a matter of the Body. You cannot serve the Lord properly as an individual Christian. To serve the Lord, you need to realize that the Lord's service is something in the Body.

Every believer is a member of the Body, a part of the Body. An individual is not the Body. A member of the Body cannot function without the Body. The hand is good, quite useful, but if it is cut off from the body, it becomes not only dead but also ugly, terrible, and even terrifying. You may love to shake my hand, but if this hand were detached from the body, it would be terrible.

Today many Christians are detached, separated from the reality of the Body. It is as if they are disembodied members. The members of a body are beautiful as long as they are attached where they belong in the body, but in any other place they are terrible. How sad it is that many Christians today are like ears that have been detached and put on the shoulders. How could they serve the Lord? How could we serve the Lord without being built up together as members of the Body? It is impossible.

I am not speaking on this point according to knowledge or doctrine. By the mercy of the Lord, I can testify to you from my experience that for many years I have simply been unable to serve the Lord without the Body. It is impossible to serve the Lord without the Body, without the church life, without the church practice.

The Body life is in Romans 12, and the church service is in this Body life with the members of the Body, of the church, functioning, serving. This matter is very clear in the Word. We need to check ourselves to see whether or not we have the reality of the Body life. If not, we are wandering saints. If you say that you are in the reality of the Body, you need to consider seriously where the Body is, practically speaking. If we could give up the service of the Lord, there would be no need for us to talk about the Body, the church life. But if we do have the sincere heart to serve the Lord, we need to realize that the service is in the Body.

THE PRIESTHOOD AND THE BODY

The Christian service is the service of the priests. We know that all the believers are priests and that the function, the duty, the responsibility, of the priests is to serve the Lord. The service of the priests in the Old Testament was not that of individual priests serving the Lord. All the priests serving the Lord need to be built up together as a body. The priestly service is not a service of individuals but a service of a corporate body. To serve the Lord, we need to be built up together with others as a corporate body. Peter told us that we will be the priesthood after we have been built up together as the spiritual house (1 Pet. 2:5).

BUILT UP AND COORDINATED

The Greek word rendered *priesthood* is rather hard to translate. But according to the spiritual reality, the priesthood is the building up of the priests, the coordination, the cooperation of all the priests. Not one of the priests serves individually, but all serve in coordination.

While I am ministering, my whole body is serving in a coordination. My mouth does not speak without any expression in my eyes or without any gestures with my hands. The mouth even needs the feet with the legs and the whole body to support it. The mouth needs the hands and feet, and the hands and feet need the mouth and the eyes. This is the whole body in coordination, and this is the basic principle of the Christian service.

Many of us are concerned about the gospel preaching. If we are going to preach the gospel, we need to be built up together. We need the coordination first. When we are built up together as a spiritual house and have the coordination of the priests, then we can preach the gospel.

The first gospel preaching was on the day of Pentecost, when one hundred twenty people were built up together, coordinated. Those one hundred twenty people were one hundred twenty priests, just as one body acting in coordination. I believe that on that day, when Peter stood up, it was not only Peter himself, nor even Peter with the other eleven, but actually Peter with the one hundred twenty. When Peter told the Jewish people, "You people put this Jesus on the cross," I believe all the one hundred twenty said, "Amen!" When he said, "You put Him to death, but the God of our fathers raised Him up," again they said, "Amen!" It was not merely a single member of the Body, not merely the mouth of Peter speaking, with all the others sleeping or talking, leaving poor Peter to speak in a poor way by himself. This is not the way the gospel was preached on that day. Rather, they preached the gospel in a prevailing way, in a coordination of all the saints, all coordinated as one. Therefore, their preaching was powerful and prevailing.

To have the gospel preached in a prevailing way, spiritual giants or powerful evangelists are not so much needed as the Body, a built-up Body under a coordination. Groups of people will be brought to the Lord through the built-up church. If we would all be joined together in the Body and stand together, even the weakest one among us would be stronger in the coordination than any individual strong one.

Some may be concerned that they do not have a special gift or do not know how to serve the Lord. Those things do not matter. As long as we are in the reality of the Body, that is wonderful. We all need to be built up in the Body. If we become a built-up house, then we will be a serving priesthood, a serving priestly coordination. This is what we need, a coordination by building up.

HOLY PRIESTS AND ROYAL PRIESTS

We are the holy priesthood on the one hand, and the royal priesthood on the other hand. In the Old Testament types there are two different orders of priests, the order of Aaron and the order of Melchisedec. The order of Aaron is the holy order. To be holy is to be separated from the common things, the worldly things, unto the Lord. The holy order is an order separated from the world, from the common things, unto the use of the Lord. To have the church service, all of us need to be built together, and we should be separated people, separated from the world, from the common things, from the ordinary way. To be separated unto God is to be holy unto God. To be holy simply means to be sanctified, and to be sanctified simply means to be separated from the common things unto the divine things. This is the holy order, the holy priesthood.

The order of Melchisedec is the royal order. Melchisedec was a king, and he was a kingly priest. On one hand, we are the sons of Aaron, the holy priests separated from the world unto the Lord. On the other hand, we are Melchisedecs, the kingly priests.

Let me illustrate in this way. Suppose the church here is going to preach the gospel. First of all, we need to be built up together as one Body; we must be formed together as an army. Then we all should be separated from the world unto the Lord. We all need to go to the Lord and pray for a period of time, like those one hundred twenty in Acts who prayed for ten days. They separated themselves from the worldly things unto the Lord, and they stayed with the Lord for ten days. As a result, they were all filled with the Lord. At that moment they were the holy priests. After those ten days, when they came out to the people to tell them that Jesus is the Lord, the Savior, they did this in a royal way. When they went to the Lord, they were holy. When they came out from the presence of the Lord with the heavenly authority, they were kings; they were royal.

When we are built up together, separated from the world unto the Lord, and we pray before the Lord, we will be the holy priests. After much prayer, we all will be filled with the Lord, even filled with the Lord of authority. Then we come out to tell the people something about the Lord as royal priests, kingly priests, with the heavenly authority. When we as the Body go to the Lord and remain in His presence, we are the holy priests, the holy, separated ones before God. After we pray and are burdened by the Lord and equipped with the heavenly authority, we come out of the presence of the Lord to the people, serving them, even ministering the Lord to them. At that time we are the kingly priests, the royal priests, the heavenly ones with the heavenly authority as heavenly kings to minister the Lord to others. What comes out is not merely preaching of the word, of the gospel, but preaching the gospel with the kingly, heavenly authority.

The priests of the order of Aaron always bring the need of the people to God. They are holy. But a priest of the order of Melchisedec brings something from God to supply others, to meet the need of others. This is the kingly priesthood.

When we give up the whole world and go to the Lord to pray for sinners, "Lord, be merciful, remember them, save them, deliver them," we are the holy priests. But when we come out of the presence of the Lord after much prayer to minister something of the Lord as life in a powerful way, in a way of heavenly authority, we are royal priests.

THREE VITAL MATTERS

If we are going to serve the Lord in the way of the church service, we need to pay our full attention to these three matters. First we need to be built up as a Body. You cannot have any service outside the church life, outside the Body. You need to be built up.

Second, each one of us needs to exercise to put everything worldly aside. We should be separated from the common things unto the Lord and learn how to remain in the presence of the Lord, how to bring the need of the people, the need of the sinful world, to the Lord and pray. Then we will be the holy priests.

After offering sufficient prayer to the Lord, we will come out from the presence of the Lord to minister the Lord to the world as the Savior, the life, the life supply, and the light in a powerful way. At that very moment we will be the royal priests. There is the need of coordination, the need of separation, and the need of the heavenly authority. We need the coordination of the Body, the separation of the holy priests from the world unto the Lord, and the heavenly authority of the royal priests. Then we will be qualified, empowered, to minister the Lord to others as the royal priests, the kingly priests, with the heavenly authority. To have the real church service, these three things are basic, even vital.

If you have a burden to minister a word to the church, first you need to check whether you have been built up in the reality of the Body and are in the coordination. If not, it is as if you are a detached member. How then could you function?

Then you need to check whether you are separated unto the Lord, and check whether you have spent sufficient time in the presence of the Lord to pray. Without this, you are not qualified to serve, because you are not a holy priest.

Then check the third item: Do you have the authority, the heavenly authority? Do you have something really committed unto you by the Lord? If so, you will minister to the Lord's people not only by word but by authority. Whenever or whatever you minister, there will be the weight. The message, the word, the ministry, will be weighty because there is the heavenly authority of the royal priest.

The coordination, the separation, and the authority— these three are the qualifications, the equipment we need to minister. It is not merely a matter of knowing something or having a burden to do something. You need to check whether you have been built up in the reality of the Body, whether you are in the coordination of the priesthood. This is something vital. You can never stand by yourself against the evil forces of darkness. The evil forces, the evil spirits, know where you are.

In Acts 19:13-16, the seven sons of Sceva attempted to cast out the evil spirits by using the name of the Jesus that Paul preached. However, the evil spirit told them, "Jesus I know of, and with Paul I am acquainted; but who are you?" The name of Jesus in the mouth of Paul is powerful, but it may not be powerful in your mouth. Paul was coordinated, built up together, with the saints. He was in the coordination of the priesthood, and he had the separation and the authority.

Even to offer a prayer in a prayer meeting or around the Lord's table, you need these three basic things: the coordination, the separation, and the authority. If you are one in the coordination of the saints, separated from the world unto the Lord, and one with the heavenly authority, when you pray just a short word, others will sense dominion, power, and reality in your prayer. Otherwise, you pray in vain words, without weight, without power, authority, to back up your words.

The real service, the prevailing service, does not depend upon knowledge, ability, eloquence, or so-called gifts. Although these things have a certain place in the service of the Lord, they are not basic. The basic matters are these three: coordination, separation, and authority.

If you would be willing to be built up together with others, simply lose yourself, let yourself be lost, in the building of the church. When you give up yourself to realize the building of the church, you are in the coordination. Then you realize the separation with the saints from the world unto the Lord, and you do have the authority of the heavens. This is the way to have the church service that is powerful and prevailing.

Peter was just an unlearned fisherman. Before the day of Pentecost I doubt that Peter had any gift. But on the day of Pentecost Peter was one in the coordination and was one with the separation and the heavenly authority. How powerful he was! He spoke a brief word with short sentences, without much knowledge, but his word was full of power. He had the coordination, the separation, and the authority. He was in the coordination, he was one of the holy priests, and he was one of the royal priests.

When those one hundred twenty people stayed in the presence of the Lord for ten days, all of them were the holy priests. When the day of Pentecost came, they all came out to the people to meet their need with the heavenly supply. Because they were royal priests, even the highest power on this earth was afraid of them because of their authority. They had the heavenly power with the heavenly authority.

This is the way to have the church service. Until we take care of these three basic matters—the coordination, the real separation, and the heavenly authority—we simply are not ready to begin any service in our locality. We need the building up, we need the coordination, we need the separation, and we need the heavenly authority. We need the reality of the Body, we need the holy priesthood, and we need the royal priesthood. When a group of saints is built up together as one Body in coordination, with the separation and the heavenly authority, at that time the real church service will begin.

CHAPTER TWO

SERVING IN THE SPIRIT
TO MINISTER CHRIST TO OTHERS

Scripture Reading: Rom. 7:6; 2 Cor. 3:6, 8

THREE VITAL POINTS

In the previous chapter we saw three vital points regarding the matter of service. The first is that in the church all the serving ones must be built up together as a spiritual house, the priesthood (1 Pet. 2:5).

All the Old Testament priests served the Lord in a corporate way. Not one served the Lord in an individual, independent way. They were all coordinated, and they all cooperated one with another. They were built up together as one body. By that Old Testament type we know that the New Testament saints need to be built up together as a spiritual house and that this spiritual house is a body of priests, a priesthood.

The priesthood is a building up of all the priests, all the serving ones, as one body. Among them there is a priesthood, a priestly body, a corporation, a coordination of a group of believers built up together, serving the Lord. To serve the Lord we first need to be built up together.

Second, we should be the holy priesthood, the separated ones, the saints, the believers, the serving ones, separated from the system of the world unto God, unto the service of the Lord. We need to be separated so that we can be holy.

Then we need to be the royal priesthood. We have seen the difference between the holy priesthood and the royal priesthood. The holy priesthood is a group of serving ones who have been separated from the satanic system of the world unto the service of God. The royal priesthood is a group of priests, a group of serving ones, who have spent time in the presence of the Lord, who have been anointed and committed with the heavenly authority. They are the Lord's ruling channel with heavenly authority. When they come out of the presence of God to the people, they come with heavenly authority as royal priests.

On one hand, the priests are holy; on the other hand, they are royal. They are those separated unto God, and they are those committed with heavenly authority to serve the Lord. Because they are separated from the world and entrusted with heavenly authority, they are qualified and equipped to serve the Lord. These three points we have seen already.

LEARNING TO SERVE IN THE SPIRIT

Now we come to a crucial point; that is, we need to learn how to serve in the spirit. This is the fourth point in the church service. Romans 7:6 says, "But now we have been discharged from the law, having died to that in which we were held, so that we serve in newness of spirit and not in oldness of letter." We need to learn to serve in the spirit—not in the letter, not in the law, not in doctrine, but in the spirit.

Second Corinthians 3:6 indicates that the New Testament service is a matter of the Spirit, not of the letter: "Who has also made us sufficient as ministers of a new covenant, ministers not of the letter but of the Spirit; for the letter kills, but the Spirit gives life." Verse 8 continues, "How shall the ministry of the Spirit not be more in glory?"

Our Regenerated Spirit

I am afraid that many believers simply do not know what it means to serve in the spirit. Before we were saved, we were dead in our spirit. On one hand, we were very active in the mind and in the emotion, yet we were dead in the spirit. But, praise the Lord, at the time we were saved, the Lord regenerated our spirit and made it alive. From that time, we need to learn to live, to walk, to act in the spirit, not in the mind or emotion, not in the soul.

We need to learn not only to walk, to live, in the spirit but also to serve in the spirit and to serve in the newness of the spirit. My burden is to help you know something in a practical way, not in the way of doctrine or theory.

What does it mean to serve the Lord in the spirit and in the newness of the spirit? A spirit has been created within us, and we have been regenerated. Our spirit has been renewed, and the Spirit of God is now dwelling in this quickened, renewed spirit. Therefore, our spirit is now a strong factor in our being. Because this spirit has been renewed and made alive, and because it has been strengthened by the indwelling of the Holy Spirit, it surely is a strong factor in our being. Yet, due to the fact that we lack the proper teaching, we simply do not realize that we have such a renewed spirit with the Holy Spirit indwelling it. However, we should have some realization because of all the speaking in the ministry concerning this matter.

We need to walk, to live, in this spirit. We are not speaking of the Holy Spirit, but of our renewed spirit in which the Holy Spirit dwells. To walk, to live, in our spirit means that we will be in the Holy Spirit because the Holy Spirit is now indwelling our spirit. We need to live in the spirit, and we need to learn to serve in the spirit.

Choosing a Hymn in the Spirit

Suppose you plan to choose a hymn for a meeting. There are two ways to choose a hymn—the way in the letter, and the way in the spirit. Suppose on the Lord's Day morning we are having a morning service in the way of the letter, and we have one to take charge of the service. We have invited another one to come to give us a sermon. Before the service you may find out what topic that one will use for his sermon. From this you consider what hymns we should sing, perhaps two or three, and you write all the hymn numbers on the board for everyone to see when they come. This is a way in the letter.

You may think that you would never do anything in such a way in our meetings. But at least in principle you may have this kind of practice in the meetings. For the prayer meeting, you may look in the index of the hymnal and select a good hymn related to prayer just according to the letter. A way in the letter is a way of death.

Then what is the other way to choose a hymn? There is a way that is not according to your mind, your mentality, but according to the inner feeling of your spirit. You need to exercise to sense the inner feeling of the spirit. If there is no inner feeling for a certain hymn, you should not select it. When you have a proper hymn, you will sense it by the inmost feeling of your spirit.

Ministering a Word in the Spirit

We need to learn not to act or serve according to knowledge, but to act and serve according to the inmost feeling. Suppose you are going to give a message in the meeting. You need to learn the lesson not just to speak according to your knowledge.

The first time I was asked to speak before a large congregation was in 1927. I was a young man, about twenty-two years of age. I prepared a sermon and practiced for quite a number of days. I went to the seashore and practiced giving the sermon to the ocean. Then I went to the pulpit on the Lord's Day morning and delivered that message according to the mentality. Afterwards, I realized I had forgotten a good portion of it. Later on, I found out that my way was absolutely a way in the letter. That was something dead. At that time I was so young, so immature. I simply did not know how to minister in the spirit.

Gradually, however, the Lord brought me to a point where I had to minister in the spirit, according to the spirit, not according to the mentality or to knowledge. I can testify to you that many times in the past years, even on the way to the meeting, I did not know what to minister, simply because I was planning to serve in the spirit. When the hymns and prayers were over, I had to stand up to minister. While I was standing to speak, even while I was speaking the words, "Let us read," up to this point I myself did not know what to read. I spoke slowly, "Let us read." While I was pronouncing the word *read* so slowly, there was a feeling—a book, a chapter, a verse. While I was reading that portion, there was some anointing within me. Word by word, sentence by sentence, the message came out, not according to the mentality, but according to the anointing. Oh, that is wonderful and that is powerful! I cannot tell you how many times this has happened.

Offering a Prayer in the Spirit

Likewise, there are two ways to offer a prayer in the meeting. One way is to offer a prayer according to knowledge, according to a routine, much like coming to an office to do routine work. Sometimes I have an impression when certain brothers are praying that it is as if they have come to the office to do their routine work. We need to forget about all kinds of routine, all kinds of knowledge, and all kinds of letters. When we come together to pray, we need to exercise our spirit to sense the inner anointing. We should not pray according to knowledge or routine, but according to the inner feeling, the inmost feeling of the anointing.

Many times we can sense when a brother is ministering in letters. We can also sense when a brother is ministering from the anointing, when he is ministering in the spirit. In such a case we can sense something living, something anointing, something enlightening, not merely something of teaching. The same is true of prayer. By the inner sense we know when a brother or sister is praying in the spirit or merely praying in the letter, according to knowledge.

Many times, when I was praying together with some living ones who prayed in the spirit, after just one sentence I had to say, "Amen," because there was a deep echo in my spirit to their prayer in the spirit. I could not hold back my "amen" because something was burning within me. When anyone utters a prayer from the spirit, there is a spontaneous expression of agreement from the spirit of the others.

Some Christians would not agree with the saying of "amen" while others are praying. Within them there is an "amen," but they suppress it; they would not release it simply because of their opinion. But whether they would utter it or not, when anyone prays in the spirit, there is always an echo in the spirit of others.

However, many times a brother prays in the mentality, in

knowledge, in the letter, in the mind, and brings in death. The more he prays, the more people are deadened. When we are praying, we need to sense whether there is an echo in the spirit of others. When there is no echo, we need to close the prayer right away. We need to learn how to exercise our spirit while we are serving and learn how to serve in the spirit.

Visiting the Saints in the Spirit

When you are going to visit one of the saints, you need to learn to visit in the spirit. Whenever you meet another saint, there is a serious need for the exercise of the spirit. Merely talking according to your mentality, according to your knowledge, does not edify others in the spirit. You need to learn to exercise your spirit, to sense the anointing within you and to follow it. Because you have a renewed spirit which is indwelt by the Holy Spirit, you have the anointing within you. You need to take care of this anointing and fellowship with the saints according to the inner feeling, the inner sense. Then you will serve and have fellowship with the saints in the spirit and not in the letter.

We need to consider some details because this matter is very important. Suppose a sister you are visiting opens herself to you concerning her family problems. To tell her something according to the teachings of the Scriptures does not work. During the very time you are listening to her, you need to exercise your spirit to sense her spirit and to sense the anointing within you. If you would do this, while you are listening on the one hand and sensing on the other hand, the anointing, the Holy Spirit within you, will reveal to you something so spiritual and so heavenly. Then you will be able to help her in a living way. At that very moment, you need to forget your knowledge of the Scriptures, your knowledge of the Christian teachings, and give up that knowledge. You need to exercise your spirit, looking to the Lord. While you are listening, you need to fellowship with the Lord and to sense both what is in her spirit and what is the anointing in your spirit. This is the way.

Preaching the Gospel in the Spirit

We all need to learn to practice, to exercise, and to conduct ourselves in the spirit in the service of the Lord. Suppose we are preaching the gospel. We need much more exercise in the spirit. We should not preach merely according to the gospel truths or according to the knowledge of the gospel. Merely to preach that we are all sinners and that the Lord Jesus is the Son of God who died on the cross for our sins does not work. That is the preaching in letters. Our preaching must be in the spirit.

We need some experiences to illustrate this point. Many times in the gospel preaching I have spoken a word that exactly met the need of someone who was listening, although I had no knowledge of the situation. I have described their case and exactly what they had done, along with their feelings and reactions step by step. Such a speaking has been used of the Lord to bring the needy ones to Him.

In one gospel meeting after we had taken the way of preaching according to the inner feeling of the spirit, while I was speaking, I felt I should say, "You say you are not a sinner? I tell you, you stole the chalk from the school." A few days later I learned that a young high school student had been brought to that meeting by his mother. While I was speaking, he was thinking, "Well, I am not a sinner. I haven't committed any sins." Just as he was saying this to himself, I spoke the words, "You say you are not a sinner? You stole the chalk from the school." He had actually stolen chalk from the school, but when he heard these words, he said to himself, "That doesn't matter." At that very moment I said, "You say that doesn't matter? You brought this chalk home and drew circles upon the floor." This statement caused him to tremble because that was exactly what he had done. As a result, he was saved. Later he asked his mother whether someone had told me his story and how I could have known everything he had done. Actually, I did not even know his name or anything he had done. We have had other experiences similar to this one.

Another time in the gospel preaching I turned to a particular part of a large congregation and said, "You say you are a good person? Just look how cruel you are. Your husband works hard to earn a living for you, and at the end of the year you forced him to buy a pair of high-heeled shoes for you. He did not have the money, but you forced him to do it." A week later, one of the sisters who did the visitation work told us that a young lady was saved by that word. At first that word had made her very angry because she thought her neighbor had reported her story to me and that I had scorned her publicly. When she learned that this was not the case, that young lady was convinced by the Lord.

In an illustration on another occasion I said, "Suppose you are seventy-six years of age." Later I learned of someone just that age who received the help. There are living stories of such experiences in the gospel preaching according to the inner feeling of the spirit.

We all need to learn to serve in the spirit, not in knowledge or in the letter. If we take this way, many times while we are serving in the spirit, the Holy Spirit will be so living to us.

Whenever you stand up to speak, you need to forget about your knowledge. On one hand, you need the knowledge, but when you stand up to serve, you should forget the knowledge. If you would keep your knowledge in your memory at that time, you will do much damage, and you will hinder the Spirit. While you are speaking, you need to forget about your knowledge and come back to the spirit to minister in the spirit. This is a lesson which requires much exercise. You may think that you will not know what to say if you let go of your knowledge. This may be true, but all of us need to exercise to serve, to minister, in the spirit.

MINISTERING CHRIST IN THE PRACTICAL SERVICE

The purpose of all we do in the church service is to minister Christ to others. Everything we do should minister life to others. This is the fifth point in the church service.

Suppose you come to the meeting hall to take care of some practical matters, to arrange the chairs, to do some cleaning work, or to take care of the kitchen. Whatever you are doing, you should take that as an opportunity to minister Christ to others. If you are cleaning, your cleaning should minister life to others. You need to minister Christ by cleaning. If you are teaching, your teaching should minister life to others. Merely to minister some knowledge to others is not enough. You need to minister Christ by teaching. It is the same with cooking. Even by cooking you should minister Christ.

The Way to Minister Christ

An illustration may help us understand how to minister Christ by taking care of all the practical things. In 1948 there was a conference in Shanghai with many co-workers from many places throughout the whole country, and there was a fellowship dinner for all the co-workers with the local saints. A very capable sister, who was at that time a head nurse in a large hospital, took care of many things related to the serving, the preparing, the cooking, and the arranging. She was very strong in character, and she was very prominent in everything that was done for the whole evening. Yet no one could sense Christ in her. She was highly qualified, and she did many good things, yet nothing of life was ministered through her, and the saints did not receive help from her.

Another sister was serving at that same dinner, and she was the only one of the serving ones who did anything wrong. She did something seriously wrong, and everyone there realized what she had done. Yet in this sister everyone could sense Christ. She had learned something of Christ, how to live in Christ, how to act in Christ, and even how to adjust her wrongdoings in Christ. All the co-workers there were helped by the one who did something seriously wrong, but they were not helped by the capable sister who did so many good things. It is possible to do many things in the Lord's service and yet have nothing of Christ ministered through you or by you.

The Goal and the Means

There are many lessons to learn in ministering Christ to others by cleaning, by cooking, and by doing many different practical things. It seems that we are so spiritual, so Christ-like, when we come together for a meeting, but when we are in the kitchen it seems that we are anything but Christ-like.

We need to learn the lesson to serve others and to serve God by ministering Christ to others no matter what we are doing. If you are in the spirit when you are playing the piano, by playing the piano you will minister Christ to others. As the church we are here to do nothing else but minister Christ to others. To cook a good meal for the saints, to prepare a good place for meeting, to play the piano in a skillful way—none of these things are meaningful unless they minister Christ to others. Whatever we do in the service of the Lord should minister Christ to others. We have much to learn in this matter.

In Shanghai there was an elderly sister who was very much with the Lord. It was her habit to invite the young missionary ladies who had just come to China to have tea with her in the afternoon. By serving tea to those young missionaries, this sister ministered Christ to them. A number of those young sisters could testify how much the life of the Lord was ministered to them by the serving of that tea. This sister did not teach them or say anything to adjust them, but she ministered life to those younger ones.

At one time some of those young missionaries were wearing stylish dresses, with the skirts a little too short. This elderly sister invited them to tea. While they were drinking tea, several times this sister pulled her skirt down so that she was more fully covered. Finally the other sisters began to check their own skirts. Without a word being spoken, those young ladies received a great adjustment. To serve tea was not the purpose of this elderly sister. It was simply the means by which Christ could be ministered.

To minister Christ as life to others should be the purpose of all the things we do, whether we are cleaning, arranging, cooking, visiting, ministering the Word, singing, or praying. All the practical things in the church life are nothing but the channels, the means through which, by which, and in which we would minister Christ to others.

If others cannot sense Christ in the kitchen while you are cooking, it is doubtful that they will sense Him in the meetings in a real way. To have Christ ministered in the meetings, we need to exercise ourselves in such a way in doing all the practical things that Christ will be ministered in the practical things. Every part of the service of the church must minister Christ as life.

We need to learn to serve in the spirit, and we need to learn to do all the things in the service of the church in a way that ministers Christ to others. This is our aim and purpose.

Unless we learn the lessons in these matters, the church life will be damaged, and death will be brought in through the practical matters. On the one hand, the saints may be taking care of the practical things together, but on the other hand, they may be talking nonsense or gossiping. The channels of talking and gossiping during the church service will bring death into the church life and scatter the death if the saints do not learn to serve in the spirit and minister Christ to one another. In that case, the more the saints come together for the practical service, the more the church life will be damaged.

May we all learn to minister Christ as life to others whenever we come together to serve in the church life. May we all learn to serve in the spirit to minister Christ as life to others.

CHAPTER THREE

SERVING IN COORDINATION

Scripture Reading: Rom. 7:6

We have already seen that we need to serve the Lord in the spirit, and that in our service the one thing we need to do is to minister Christ to others as life. Whatever we do in the Lord's service, we must do it in the spirit. In Romans 7:6 we are told that we need to serve the Lord not only in the spirit, but also in the newness of the spirit: "But now we have been discharged from the law, having died to that in which we were held, so that we serve in newness of spirit and not in oldness of letter."

There is at least some difference between the spirit and the newness of the spirit. However, if you serve the Lord in the spirit, you will surely have the newness of the spirit. Anything in the flesh is old; anything in the spirit is new. Whenever a brother or a sister serves in the flesh, there is a sense of something old, even six thousand years old, as old as Adam. But when anyone serves in the spirit, there is something new, something fresh and refreshing.

A good number of times I have seen the brothers and sisters who are quite young serve in an old way. There are some nineteen year olds who serve as if they were ninety-nine years old. Their serving is old because they serve in the flesh. On the other hand, some older brothers and sisters serve in a way that is fresh and new. They serve in a new way, a refreshing way, because they serve in the spirit. Whatever is in the spirit is fresh, new, and refreshing. Whatever is in the flesh is old. It is not refreshing, but rather it is tiring.

When you are listening to a message that is given in the spirit, you simply do not care about the time. After listening for half an hour, you want to hear more. The time goes by quickly. But when you are listening to a message given in the flesh, in the oldness of the letter, ten minutes may seem like an hour, and you are relieved when the message is over. All of us need to learn to serve in the spirit and in the newness of the spirit.

It is necessary to be mature, but we should never be old. To be old is one thing; to be mature is another. We should seek to be mature, but never to be old. God is never old. On the contrary, He is always new. In the Bible the Lord's maturity is portrayed in one way, and His newness is pictured in a different way, but the Lord is never old. Therefore, we should learn to serve in the spirit and in the newness of the spirit.

Whatever you do, you need to do it in the newness of the spirit. Whatever you do, you need to do it in the way of ministering Christ as life to others. You should not minister doctrines, religion, rules, regulations, or forms. You should not even minister any kind of sound teachings to others without Christ as life. Our goal is to minister Christ as life to others. We take care of sound teachings simply because those teachings have much to do with the matter of Christ as life. If doctrines and teachings are not related to Christ as life, we would not take care of them and would not talk about them.

We need to learn to serve in the spirit, and we need to minister Christ as life to others. These two matters we have seen.

THE WAY OF COORDINATION

There is more to say about serving in the newness of the spirit and ministering life to others. However, in this chapter my burden is another point of the service, that is, the matter of coordination. In the service we need to be coordinated with others. I do not say that we need to be organized. To be organized is one thing, and to be coordinated is another. What we mean by the word *coordination* is simply to be built up together and to serve in the way of being built up together.

The more you serve, the more you will be built up together with others. In these days we are talking about the building up of the church. The building up of the church is in the service of coordination. If we are serving the Lord in the way of coordination, while we are serving we are being built together.

We need to see what this means in a practical way. Suppose I am one serving the Lord among the saints in the church. I need to serve the Lord in such a way that the more I serve, the more I will be built up together with others, and the more I serve, the more others will be brought in to be built up together with me. In other words, the more I serve, the more the church is built up.

In many places today, however, the more the people serve, the more they become independent. The more gifted they are, the more they become a giant, and the more they become independent. Some of the gifted ones would think that they are so high that others cannot follow them. They consider themselves so high and everyone else so low. They would put themselves on the top and others on the bottom. As a result, they would be independent. This is not the right way.

The right way is that while you are serving, you are being built together with others. The more you serve, the more you exercise your gift, the more you will be united, the more you will be coordinated with others. In the Lord's service you never act in an independent way. Here there are lessons for us to learn.

Let me illustrate in this way. Suppose I am a brother with a gift, and the more I serve, the more I will learn, and the more I will know how to serve. The more I serve, the more I will become strong, and the more I will become great. Then I will become proud, thinking that I know this, I know that, I know everything. Therefore I must do everything, because I am the only one who knows how to do it. In a sense, I am becoming almighty. I can do everything, and I do everything. The more I serve, the more everything comes into my pocket and everything is in my hand. The more I can do, the more I am independent, and I can do everything in my way. I have no more lessons to learn, and no one can teach me anything. In the meeting I announce the hymn, play the piano, start the hymn, lead the prayer, and do the preaching—I do everything. There is no need for anyone else. I can accomplish the whole job. I am on the top, and I am the most independent. Others may admire me as such a wonderful brother. Nevertheless, you all need to realize that this kind of brother simply damages the church life. The more he does, the more he delays the building up of the church; he even spoils and frustrates it. Since such a brother is so capable in himself, there are no lessons for him to learn, and there is no need for him to coordinate with others. This is not the right way.

LETTING THINGS PASS INTO THE HANDS OF OTHERS

The right way is this. On the first day that I come here to serve, I may do ninety percent of the things and leave ten percent in the hands of others. But after one month, I am taking care of only sixty percent, and the other thirty percent has passed into the hands of some others who have come in to serve with me. After another month, I may take care of only thirty percent, and another month later, maybe only five percent, then a little later, only one percent. The rest of the job of the service goes to all the serving brothers and sisters. One sister takes care of the piano. A brother takes care of the hymns. Another takes care of this, and another takes care of that. To serve the Lord in this way I need to learn many lessons. Each one of us naturally thinks that he is the best and would never let others do the same thing he does. But if you would learn the lesson to be coordinated with others, you need to learn how to look down on yourself and how to be limited by others. Otherwise, you could not bring people more and more into the building.

There was a sister in China who was quite capable, educated, and experienced in doing things, and she loved the Lord very much. However, when she came into the service of the church, the more she served, the more everything came into her hand. After two or three months, it seemed that all the others had been dismissed. One day the elders asked her why it was that there were only two or three left in the Lord's service, when a few months ago there had been quite a number. They asked where the others were. Her answer was that they did not know how to do things, and they did not do them well. The more she served, the more all the others were dismissed because of her ability and her capability. No one could work as fast as she could. In everything it seemed she was right because she was so capable. But in spiritual reality she damaged the church life very much. She acted independently. Later on, with this sister there was a great spiritual cancer.

A cancer is a part of the body that overdevelops, a group of cells that goes wild, that goes too far. You need to be limited by others so that you will not be a cancer to the Body of Christ. You need to be limited by others so that you will be a member coordinated with others, not a cell gone wild.

The best way for us to serve the Lord in the church is this way. The first week that you come to serve the Lord, you may take care of seventy percent of the things, and the others take care of thirty percent. The next week, you take sixty-five percent, and the others thirty-five percent. The third week, you may take sixty, and the others, forty. With you the percentage is always being reduced, and with the others it is always being increased.

From another angle, the first week that you come, only five percent of the saints are serving with you. After one week, there are eight percent, then twelve, twenty, and eventually, maybe after one year, one hundred percent. The percentage of the work in your hands is always being reduced, yet the number of the people serving with you is always increasing. After maybe one or two years, the service will be absolutely out of your hands and one hundred percent in the hands of all the brothers and sisters. The number of the serving ones will be increased from just a handful to more than a hundred. This is the right way.

If you take this way, you will learn to be limited, to be broken, and to submit yourself to others. If you do not serve the Lord with others, you will never know yourself, but when you serve with others, you will be exposed how "good" you really are. In this kind of service there are many lessons for you to learn.

TESTED BY THE COORDINATION

In my experience I have always been tested by the brothers in the service. This kind of testing is very hard to take, but you simply need to take it. You may tell the Lord, "Lord, this is a cup from You, and I have no choice but to take it." This is the way for you to learn the lesson of serving the Lord in the way of coordination.

When you do things by yourself, it seems that everything is convenient, but when you do things with others, it seems that nothing is convenient. For example, I would always prefer to travel by myself in the Lord's work. However, in China, under the Lord's sovereignty and under the coordination of the co-workers, I always had to travel with two or more brothers, and even to be the leader among them for the traveling. I am a person who always likes to have everything ready ahead of time, to leave nothing to be done at the last minute, and I would urge the brothers to have everything prepared for our trip. Every time there would be someone who was not ready. Eventually I would need to help him get ready, take care of things for him, and do everything for him, and we would not be ready on time. I encouraged everyone to take responsibility for their own things and not to burden others, but whatever way I tried, nothing seemed to work. Eventually I had to submit to the Lord and learn to be patient, and I had to take care of all the suitcases and all of the problems for the others. The more people you have traveling with you, the more problems you have—the luggage, the things others forget, all the special needs. You have no choice but to help. It seems that the others have come to help you, but you need to help them. They become a burden instead of a help, but they are really a help for you to learn the lesson.

One of the biggest problems is to visit a church with several co-workers to be received for hospitality by the church. Many co-workers simply do not know how to be a guest. There are many problems and many lessons for us to learn in the coordination.

What should you do in all these situations? You cannot dismiss your co-workers and send them home. You simply need to learn the lesson in the coordination. This is the only way for you to serve the Lord with others to build up the church. You should not be a giant. You should not be the one who is on the top. You always need to be coordinated with others. If you will try this way, you will surely see where you are. It is not so easy.

We are always ready to dismiss others. When some matters of the service were assigned to certain brothers or sisters, many times they would say that they wanted to make it clear that no one should come to the place where they were to serve. If they were to do the cooking, they would insist that no one else come to the kitchen. On the one hand, this is right, but on the other hand, they needed a few not only to help them but also to be a burden to them. Otherwise, there would be no lesson for them to learn. If you have some helpers that are a burden to you in the service, then you will be limited, broken, and adjusted. You need someone to be your burden. You may be too quick, and you need someone to burden you to slow you down. Then you will learn the lesson, and you will bring people in.

SURROUNDED BY SERVING ONES
WITH THE WORK OUT OF YOUR HANDS

In serving the Lord in the way of coordination, the best test of your service is to check, after a certain time, how much of the service is in your hand and how many more people have been brought into your part of the service. After six months, if all of the service is in your hand and nearly all of the people are gone—you are almost the only one left—that is serious. You may be much better than others in doing the job. However, although the job is done in a much better way, the situation in the church life has actually become worse. By doing a better job by yourself, you have actually brought damage to the church life.

You need to bring more people in, and eventually not even one percent of the work should be left in your hand. Everything should be in the hands of others, and eventually there may be hundreds of people serving with you. This is the way of coordination, the way to bring people in and to have the church built up. The more you serve, the less is in your hand. The more you serve, the larger is the number of serving ones.

You should not consider the job that you have done. Rather, you need to consider the percentage of the service that is in your hand and the number of the serving ones. There are some real lessons to be learned regarding this matter. The biggest lesson in this matter is brokenness. We may talk about being broken, but the way to be broken is to serve the Lord with your brothers and sisters in the way of coordination.

OPENNESS FOR THE COORDINATION

We do need the training in this matter, and we need the practice. What we have been talking about is mainly on the practical side. If you would take these matters and put them into practice, you will realize how much is involved here. Just this little word is enough for you to practice for your whole life. You will find that there is a nature within you that is always independent, a nature that is always secretive. You do not like to open yourself to others. Something in your blood always likes to be independent and to keep things secret, hidden from others. Some brothers and sisters are able to talk about many things without opening themselves to others. They talk, but they always keep themselves closed. You may serve the Lord with them for quite a period of time and still not know where they are.

If you would take this word to serve the Lord in a way of coordination, then you will find out where you are. By nature you are an independent person, a secretive person, even a person of mystery. You like to keep yourself hidden in yourself as a mystery. God caused the church to be hidden in Himself as a mystery in the Old Testament, but today you are keeping yourself as a mystery within yourself. It is not so easy for you to open yourself to others.

If there is no openness, this means that there is no brokenness. The more brokenness there is, the more openness there is, and the more openness, the more blending with others. Unless we learn the spiritual lesson of being broken, of being open, and of being blended with others, it will be impossible for us to have the church life. We can come together week after week, month after month, and year after year, but we can never have a church life. We can never be built up together to express Christ in a corporate way. We can never be blended as one in the spirit because our natural life, our soulish life, our human nature, has never been broken. There is only one way for you to experience the real brokenness of the natural life, and that is to be coordinated with others. You cannot merely close yourself in your room to read the Scriptures and pray and praise the Lord that you are broken. The more you declare in your room that you are broken, the more you are not broken. Whether or not you are really broken is tested by the coordination with others.

Suppose there is a sister who always likes to close herself in a room to seek after the Lord. She is very faithful to read the Word, to meditate, to kneel down to pray day by day. Her practice is very good, but the real test is whether or not this sister is really broken. It is possible for a person to be very spiritual alone with the Lord and yet never have the self broken.

Suppose that, under the Lord's sovereignty, this sister is placed in some kind of coordination and put among seven sisters. Each of the seven is a Martha, and they simply do not know how to be quiet. In fact, all they know is work and more work, doing and more doing. Sovereignly these eight are put into a situation where there is so much that needs to be done that there is no time for this dear sister to seek the Lord alone in her room. This will become a real test to her. She may even lose her temper because she has no time for this. This is a proof that she has never been broken. After passing through such a testing, how could this sister close herself in her room in her old way and praise the Lord that she is broken? Actually, the sovereignty of the Lord brought her into such a situation to show her that she has to be broken in this very matter.

The teachings among today's Christians place too much emphasis on individual spirituality, making Christians into antiques and showpieces instead of preparing them as materials for the building. God never intended that you should be individually spiritual. Individual spirituality spoils and does much damage to the building of the church. If you realize that God's eternal purpose, God's ultimate intention, is to have a Body, a corporate vessel to contain Christ and to express

Christ, you will say, "Lord, save me; deliver me from my individual spirituality. I have to be broken even in this matter of individual spirituality. I need to be delivered from this kind of individuality. I need to learn the lesson to be broken so that I could be coordinated with others, so that I could be blended with others and become a real help to them."

The proper way for such a spiritual sister to serve the Lord is to learn the lesson of brokenness, to learn how to be delivered by the Lord from her individual spirituality, to learn to go along with others. Then, gradually, the others will learn the same lesson, and this sister will be a help to them and minister the life of Christ to them in the proper way. All of these eight will then be built up together, and they will bring more and more people to be coordinated with them. Then they will be spiritual in a coordinated way, not in an individual way. Surely this is a much needed lesson.

We need to stress this matter so much simply because by experience we realize that if we would not learn this lesson, we can never have a real church life. Without this, our church life would be a false one. We can come together on the Lord's Day and sing a hymn, have some prayer, and hear a message, but that is all. We can never have a church built up. We cannot have a group of believers built up together as a living corporate Body. We need to learn to serve in a way that we could be coordinated with others and others could be coordinated with us. There are many lessons here for us to learn.

Besides brokenness, you need to learn always to make it possible for others to coordinate with you. If you all would simply take this word and go on to serve the Lord in a way of coordination, there is no need for me to say anything more. There are many lessons ahead of you, but you should not give up. The more lessons you have, the more you need to learn, and the more you learn, the more the lessons will continue to come. This is the way the Lord builds up His church.

If three persons can do a particular job in the Lord's service, you should not reduce the number to two. It would be better to have four or even five. Never reduce the number, but always increase it, because the more the number is increased, the more lessons there are for you to learn and the more the building will be realized.

Some brothers have said, "I simply cannot do anything if some sisters are here. If you would ask me to do something, you must tell these sisters not to come to me." I am afraid that we may still have some brothers in such a situation. If you are such a brother, the Lord will send you more sisters; and probably, under His sovereignty, He will send you the most troublesome ones. The Lord will test you to show you where you are. You need to learn the lesson to do the work in the service in a corporate way. The church is a test to you, and the real service of the church is also a test.

We all should try to know the church. We need to practice to know the way of the church service, which is a service of coordination, never a service of an individual person. All the service in the church is a service of coordination.

Many times I like to fellowship with the brothers about my message before I deliver it. This is the best way. It is good to come together with the brothers to fellowship about the message you are going to give, taking the attitude of being open to others and being ready to be adjusted. If the brothers would give you just a little hint that they would not have you minister, you should be willing to take it. You should not act in an independent way. In everything, in every job, in every part of the Lord's service, you need to try to open yourself to others to be coordinated with them, and to do everything in the service in a way of coordination. Then you will learn the lesson, and the church will be much profited in the matter of building up. Otherwise, we may have many meetings, but we could not have the real church life.

Chapter Four

THE RELATIONSHIP BETWEEN
THE MINISTRY AND THE CHURCH

Scripture Reading: Acts 13:1-4a

In order to serve the Lord among His children in the most proper way, we must know the relationship between the work, or the ministry, and the church. If we consider the record and the teachings in the Acts and all the Epistles in the New Testament, it is clear that the ministry is something closely related to the church yet still different from the church. The church was formed on the day of Pentecost. Before that day, there was no church in Jerusalem, but something else was there, something closely related to the church but different from it. That was the work, or the ministry, among the apostles under the leadership of Peter. Then after the church in Jerusalem was established, the ministry in the hands of the apostles with Peter was still there as something related to the church and entirely for the church but different from the church.

If we read Acts 13, we can see that in Antioch there was also a church, and there again was something related to the church and for the church yet different from the church. This was the work, the ministry, among a group of the Lord's servants, which included the apostles Paul and Barnabas. In the following chapters of Acts, the relationship between the ministry and the church is very clear. Before the churches were established in many localities, the apostle Paul went to those places to work, and it was his ministry that brought the churches into being. Then after those local churches were produced and established, the work still remained there. Therefore, from Acts 2 to the end of the book, we can clearly see that there are two things in parallel; one is the church, and the other is the ministry, the work.

It is clear that the work in the hands of the apostles under the leadership, the headship, of Paul was one hundred percent for the church, yet it was not something of the church. It was not in the hand of the church, in the government of the church, or under the direction or control of the church. The church in Antioch did not send Paul and Barnabas to the work. In the church there was no mission board to send missionaries to the foreign field. Paul and Barnabas were not under the direction of the church in Antioch; rather, they were separate from the church in Antioch. However, they were related to it, and what they went to do was completely for the local churches established around Antioch.

The apostles did not do any work for themselves; what they did was completely for the local churches. They were a group of workers of God very much related to the churches, and they worked to produce, establish, edify, and build up the churches. However, they were not of the local churches, neither of Antioch nor of any of the other churches established by them later, and they were not sent by the churches or controlled by the churches. They were separate from the churches, and their work was separate from the churches. When they went to the church meetings, they acted as members of the church. They were simply brothers in the church meetings, the same as the other brothers. As co-workers of the Lord, however, they were not apostles of the church in Antioch, of the church in Ephesus, or of any other local church.

THE MINISTRY AND THE CHURCHES
BEING DIRECTLY UNDER THE HAND OF THE LORD

The ministry, the work, has much to do with the churches and is one hundred percent for the churches, yet it is not of the church. It is not under the control or direction of the church but is directly under the control of the Head, the Lord Jesus. The principle is the same with the churches. All the churches have much to do with the ministry and the apostles, but they are not under the hand or control of the apostles; they are directly under the headship of the Lord Jesus. The ministry does not control the local churches, and the churches do not control the ministry. Both the church and the ministry are directly under the control of the Head.

It is the Lord's intention to keep human hands off the work and off the church. The Lord does not want to have His ministry under the hand of a local church. It is not right for a church to hire someone to serve the Lord and send people to work for Him. This puts the Lord's servants under the hand of men and almost makes them the servants of men. Many missionaries, for example, must submit a written resignation when they leave their field.

When I was young, a certain person in my family was a graduate from the best seminary in China, and she became a preacher. She would often speak about her job, saying, "Next year I will resign from this church and take a job in another church." We would ask her about the terms of her employment, including her salary and traveling expenses, and then we would encourage her to take the better job. However, the Lord's intention is to keep His work and His workers directly in His hands and not under human control.

In the same way, the Lord intends to keep the local churches directly in His hands. According to the first three chapters of Revelation, the Lord is the One who walks among the golden lampstands. He is the only One who supervises all the churches. All the churches are under His hand and headship. The Lord does not agree to have human hands come in. This is a very basic principle.

DISTINGUISHING THE SERVICE OF THE MINISTRY FROM THE SERVICE OF THE CHURCH

If we are going to serve the Lord, we must realize whether we are serving the Lord in the church or in the ministry. What kind of service did Timothy have? Was his service of the church, or was his service of the ministry? We may answer in this way: When he went to the church meetings simply as a brother, what he did there was a service of the church, but for the most part Timothy's service was of the ministry; it was for the church but not of the church. To serve the Lord in the service of the church is one thing, while to serve the Lord in the service of the ministry is another.

When someone learns to drive a car, he must learn many lessons. If he drives a car blindly in whatever way he likes, he will cause much damage or loss of life. To drive a car, one must know what kind of car it is, where he is going, and on what lane he should be. There are many rules to keep. In the same way, if we are going to serve the Lord, we must learn the lessons. We must come to serve the Lord in a very clear way. Many brothers and sisters seem to have the attitude that it is good enough simply to come and serve in any way. However, this will cause damage. The biggest distinction we must learn in the Lord's service is the relationship between the ministry and the church.

A local church may have a burden to train the local saints. Then they may invite some of the Lord's servants to come to help in doing this work. If so, such a training is something of the church. On the other hand, a training may be the burden not of the church but of some of the Lord's servants. The Lord's servants may be burdened to help the saints to know how to serve the Lord, how to follow the Lord, how to experience the Lord, and how to practice the church life. In this case, such a training is under the hand of the Lord's servants. It is not something of the church but of the ministry. We must differentiate these two ways.

If something is conducted by the church, it must be under the hand of the church. Whatever is done must be under the direction of the church. In this case, the workers of the ministry have no liberty to seek the Lord's mind for the direction. Rather, they must go to the leading ones in the church and ask, "Brothers, what do you want me to do for this training?" The leading ones may examine a worker to see if he properly knows the divisions and meanings of the books of the Scriptures. If he does not, they will give him another duty and find someone else to care for the training. Such a training is carried out when the church realizes what is of the Lord, for the Lord, and for the churches in the various localities. Then that church is happy to do something to help the situation in a corporate way.

A training of the ministry, however, is not carried out in this way. It is carried out through a burden directly from the Lord which He has put in the heart of the minister. It is not of a local church in a certain place but is the burden of the ministering one. Then the leading ones in the church agree that it is something for the building up of the Lord's church, and they do as much as they can to cooperate. We need to be very clear about these two ways in order to maintain the church and the work under the direct control of the Lord's hand. Otherwise, we may put the church under the hand of the work or put the work under the hand of the church. There are lessons here for us to learn.

Some have considered that our training meetings are simply church meetings, like the prayer meeting of the church. They do not realize that the church, strictly speaking, cannot conduct a work like this. It should have only the church service. The preaching of the gospel by the church, for example, is the service of the local church, but the training meetings are not of the service in a local church. Our summer conferences, for example, are also not church meetings; they are apart from the church meetings. Of course, the local churches are related to them, but those meetings are not something of the local church. They are something of the ministry to help the churches.

We should consider much before the Lord: Are we serving the Lord in the church or in the ministry? The service of the ministry is related to the service of the church, and the service of the church is related to the service of the ministry, but we cannot and should not confuse them. The training meetings we are conducting at this time are much related to the church in this locality, and the local church is very much related to the training, but these two are not one item. The service we raise up to serve the Lord in the church may be a help, a preparation, for the service of the ministry, yet we are still serving the Lord in the local church, and we must be under the local church. If we are serving the Lord in the local church, we must be under the local church, while if we serve the Lord in the ministry, we must be in the coordination of the work.

The trainings which we are conducting at this time are always kept separate from the local meetings of the church on the Lord's Day and at other times. It is a work of the ministry, separate from the church. Of course, it is for the church to help the church and the saints, but it is separate from the church. Therefore, there is no need for this ministry to give a report to the church or ask the church to support it.

Acts 13:1-4a speaks of five prophets and teachers in the church in Antioch. Strictly speaking, these prophets and teachers were not local members of the church there. Their praying together was not the prayer meeting of the local church; it was a prayer meeting of the ministry, a prayer meeting of a group of the Lord's workers. This demonstrates that if we are going to serve the Lord, we must serve Him in a right order. If we are going to serve in the service of the church, we must be under the coordination of the church, that is, under the order of the church. But if we are going to share in the service of the ministry, we must be in the coordination of the ministry.

Many saints do not consider this, however. They feel that as long as they serve the Lord, everything is all right. It is all right now, but later on they may encounter problems with themselves or with others, if they are not clear about these matters. In order to help us to serve the Lord properly, to know things properly, and to have proper relationships with all the Lord's children, we must know these matters.

Recently, some brothers as co-workers published a small booklet concerning the faith. Strictly speaking, this was not something of the church. Of course, it was for the church, to help the church and the saints, but as far as the responsibility, the burden, and the ministry are concerned, it had nothing to do with the church and was entirely outside of the church. It was part of the ministry through a few co-workers. Because we have the intention to publish more messages in booklets, we need a little bookroom, so we included the address of the bookroom in that booklet. This is one hundred percent not a church matter. This bookroom does not need to report to the church, receive directions from the church, or ask anything of the church. It is absolutely a matter of a few brothers who are co-workers in the ministry.

Each one of us must be clear about these things and must consider in what part of the Lord's service we are, in the church service or the service of the ministry. Then we will know where we are, and we will know where we must stand in the coordination. We cannot serve the Lord independently. We must be coordinated, but in order to be coordinated rightly, we must realize in what part of the service we are serving. If we are serving in the church, we must be coordinated in the church service, but if we are serving in the ministry, we must be coordinated in the service of the ministry.

I can give you only these points and principles; later on you will realize that they will help us to keep ourselves in the proper order. In the future, many churches will be built up, and we believe that many co-workers will be raised up by the Lord. There will be a great portion of the ministry, and there will be even a greater portion of the church service. Then we will need to realize our part, stand in it, and keep ourselves in order in the coordination. No human hand can arrange this. This can be carried out only by the guidance of the Holy Spirit, but we need to learn all these principles so that we can continue to serve the Lord in a very proper way and understand others in a full way. In the future, these principles and points will be helpful to us.

CHAPTER FIVE

GOSPEL PREACHING IN THE CHURCH

Scripture Reading: Matt. 28:19; Mark 16:15; Acts 2:14; Eph. 6:15

In this chapter we will see something concerning how to preach the gospel in the church. According to church history, Christians in past generations have taken many ways to preach the gospel for the Lord. However, we would like to see something from the Scriptures concerning gospel preaching. At the end of the Gospel of Matthew, the Lord told us to go and preach the gospel to the nations, making them the Lord's disciples (28:19). In the Scriptures, especially in the first three Gospels, there is the principle that Christians must be persons who go. We must go for the purpose of the gospel. In the Gospels we are called by the Lord to come, and we are commanded by the Lord to go. Christians are people who constantly come and go. We come all the time to the Lord, and we go all the time to others. We come to the Lord for mercy, grace, life, and power. However, this is half of the commandment. We also need the other half. We must go! After coming to the Lord, we must go to the nations for the gospel, to gain their souls.

BALANCING OUR CHRISTIAN LIFE
BY THE PREACHING OF THE GOSPEL

It is very strange that most Christians are not balanced persons. The Lord calls us to come to Him, but after we come, He tells us to go to the nations. However, some Christians learn how to come to the Lord all the time, but they forget to go. Of course, other Christians today are going Christians, but I am afraid that they do not come enough to the Lord.

Therefore, we must be balanced. The coming and going Christians are sound, normal Christians. On the one hand, we need to learn how to come to the Lord all the time, day by day; then on the other hand, we need to learn how to go. We come into the Holy of Holies, and we go outside the camp, to others, to the nations. If we have the intention and sincere desire to practice the church life, we must be brothers and sisters who come to the Lord day by day and go to others all the time.

When I was young, I was helped by a short but interesting writing. The writer said that in order to be a sound Christian, every day we must spend at least ten minutes to speak to the Lord, ten minutes for the Lord to speak to us, ten minutes to speak to sinners, and ten minutes to speak with the saints. Day by day we must have these four times of at least ten minutes each. This is not a small matter. Try to put it into practice. If we do this, we will be healthy in spiritual matters and in the spirit. However, we should not do too much; at the outset we should just do a little.

We need to be balanced. Even for our physical life we need many things, including eating, drinking, and clothing. It is the same in the spiritual life. We must include gospel preaching as an item to balance our Christian life. If we have not preached the gospel in several days, we are not balanced. If we are going to practice a proper church life, our church life and the Christian life of every brother and sister must be balanced by gospel preaching. In the four Gospels, whoever came to the Lord, the Lord sent him to others to preach. Matthew 28:19 tells us to go to the nations, but Mark 16:15 says that we must go even to all creation. This verse says, "And He said to them, Go into all the world and proclaim the gospel to all the creation." Christians have much to do to preach the gospel not only to the nations but also to every creature. We must do it!

PREACHING THE GOSPEL
BEING A MATTER OF THE CHURCH

In the Acts, we can see that gospel preaching is a matter of the church. It is when the church is built up that there is the impact in our preaching. After the Lord accomplished His redemption by His death and resurrection, and after He ascended, the gospel was completed. Then the first time it was preached, it was preached not by an individual but by the church. The first time the gospel was preached after the completion of the gospel was by the Body of Christ on the day of Pentecost. When Peter stood up, he stood with the eleven; twelve stood together to speak the gospel to the people. They had the oneness and the impact. No doubt, all the one hundred twenty also stood together. In this way, the entire church, consisting of one hundred twenty persons, preached the gospel. There must have been a great impact on the day of Pentecost.

The preaching of the gospel is a battle. Therefore, we need to pray. Before we plunder the strong man's vessels, we must bind him. The strong man is the enemy, Satan, whom we bind. We must fight the battle so that we can preach the gospel in a prevailing way. However, if we are not built together as one, the enemy, Satan and the evil spirits, will laugh at us because we will not have the impact. We will have lost the testimony of the Body of Christ before the enemy. If we are going to preach the gospel in a prevailing way, we must be built together as one. Even though the brothers among us are few, if we would be one in the spirit and built together as one, we eventually will have the impact. However, if there are divisions among us, if we have opinions and quarrel with one another, the impact of the gospel preaching will be gone. This is something that transpires in the spiritual world. In any kind of world there are always certain principles. In the spiritual world with the preaching of the gospel, there is the principle of the oneness of the Body. If we are not one, we simply lose the impact, the power, and the authority to preach the gospel.

CONSECRATING OURSELVES FOR THE GOSPEL

We need to help all the brothers and sisters learn how to pray, on the one hand, and learn how to preach, on the other hand. However, this does not mean that we give people a sermon. In order to help the brothers and sisters to preach the gospel, we must help them to consecrate themselves again. Even though they may have consecrated themselves many times, they still need to consecrate themselves once again purposely and specifically for this matter. This is absolutely according to the principle of the teachings of the Scriptures. The Scriptures teach us that whenever we are going to do something specifically, we need to consecrate ourselves again for that very specific purpose. We may ask the brothers to come together to have a meeting for some prayer to offer themselves to the Lord for this purpose.

CONSIDERING OUR RELATIVES, NEIGHBORS, FRIENDS, SCHOOLMATES, AND COLLEAGUES

It is helpful to consider before the Lord all the names of our relatives, neighbors, friends, schoolmates, and colleagues, and all the persons with whom we are familiar, and it is better to write these names down. Then we should consider how many of them are already Christians and truly saved, and if possible, we should pray for them. In this prayer, the Lord may lead us to do something, perhaps not for all of them but for a few of them. There are many details to consider. We should consider whom to visit and whom to write, sending them gospel tracts, booklets, and helpful messages. We should invite some of these persons to our homes to eat. If we have friends or relatives in other cities, we can mail them something and tell them where the meeting place is in their city. We can also ask the brothers there to visit them. We should first take care of the persons with whom we are familiar. This is our responsibility, and we should carry this out not once for all but all the time, year after year.

THE NEED FOR THE CHURCH TO BEAR FRUIT

The first commission from the Lord to the church is to preach the gospel, to bring new believers to the church. I met a group of brothers and sisters who considered themselves to be the most spiritual persons in their locality. They were very nice, spiritual, and everything about them was good. However, I asked them, "Brothers, how long have you been meeting in this way, and with how many persons did you start to meet?" They said that they had been meeting for a long time and that they had started with about twenty persons, the same number they had when I spoke with them. Whenever they came together, they were very nice and spiritual, but they had no fruit, no converts. This is wrong.

How can a tree not bring forth fruit if it is truly living? As a church, we must be prevailing in winning souls. We need to check ourselves by many ways to see if we are right or wrong; one way to check ourselves is by whether or not we bring forth fruit. The number of the members of the church must increase all the time. New converts must be added to the church constantly. I hope that the churches will bring forth fruit in the next half year. Then that will be our "fruit season." If we do not bring forth fruit, there must be something wrong with us. We cannot and should not gather together week after week, singing hymns and listening to good messages, but after one, two, or even three years not bringing in new converts. If so, there is something wrong with the church, and there is also something wrong with the believers.

A necessary item for training young believers is to help them to promise to bring one person to the Lord each year. Some need to promise to bring two or four persons a year to the Lord, and one saint may even promise to bring ten persons. If they promise, they will do it. If every brother or sister brings one new convert to the church each year, the entire world will be evangelized in about thirty years. The first year we will start with one hundred, then the next year we will have two hundred, and each year we will double again. If we just do it, it will be easy to bring one person to the Lord in three hundred sixty-five days.

We need the ways to carry this out. As I have said, the first way is to consider our relatives, neighbors, and all the persons with whom we are familiar. If we will consider in this way, I am sure that we can bring one person to the Lord each year. When D. L. Moody was young, he made the decision to speak to one person about Jesus each day. One day after he went to bed, he remembered that he had not told anyone about the Lord that day. He went out, but since it was late in the night, he could find only a policeman. The policeman asked him what he was doing, and Moody told him he must believe in Jesus. The policeman was angry with Moody, but eventually he was saved.

I do not like to speak about myself, but I must tell you that when I was about twenty-five years old, I always carried gospel tracts in my pocket. When I walked on the street, I distributed them whenever there was the opportunity. Some fruit came out of that practice. We should encourage the young brothers and sisters to carry tracts in their pockets and distribute them in order to contact people. By doing this, they will eventually bring someone to the Lord. At the least, this will create the atmosphere of the gospel. There are many ways to preach the gospel, if we would just do it.

CREATING AN ATMOSPHERE OF THE GOSPEL

When we first came to Taiwan in 1949, many of us were poor. We did not know how we would live after another two or three months. We did not have much, but I told the saints that we still should use some of our money to prepare tracts and posters. We prepared many posters, and just within one month we distributed two-thirds of a million tracts, which was as many tracts as there were people. We distributed them in all the lanes, roads, and streets and at every door. We used a map to systematically go to every door. We also put posters on the electric poles in the streets, which said, "God so loved the world," "Jesus saves," and other phrases in bold characters. Within a short time, we created the atmosphere of the gospel, and we stirred up nearly the whole city. At every door, without exception, there was at least one tract in the letter box telling people that the Lord Jesus is their Savior, and nearly in every street there were posters on the walls. We also asked the saints to place many posters in front of their own doors. When we walked on the street, we knew which homes the brothers lived in because of the number of posters.

All this happened in the first year, in 1949. We did many things. We formed gospel teams, and the brothers wore long white "gospel robes" with bold characters in Chinese. We also had parades with drums; at one time we had a parade nearly every week. We paraded through the streets with a large number of saints, and sometimes we prayed on the street. While we paraded on the street, sometimes we would shout, "Friends, we must tell you that you are sinners, and you need to believe in Jesus." We preached the gospel in the park in the center of the city, where there is a stadium that seats several thousand people, and we used the gospel parades to bring people to the park. All the saints came together to preach the gospel in this way every Lord's Day afternoon.

In one year the church increased thirtyfold, and the whole city was stirred up by us. Doctors, nurses, and professors paraded together in long robes; everyone knew that we were the "crazy" people. Nearly everyone talked about us in their homes. After this, it was very easy to preach the gospel because we stirred up the gospel atmosphere. What we did tilled the ground. In principle, we should do these things. Recently I asked the brothers in one church, "Why can we not see any activity for the gospel here? Even if you have only thirty or forty persons, you all must go out to the street to distribute tracts."

In 1948 in Shanghai we had the largest gospel team, and we paraded on the street on the Lord's Day. The police on the streets maintained the order for us. They stopped the buses, cars, and trains. We had banners in our hands, and we shouted much. Then we brought people to the park, and many of them knelt down to pray, some with crying to the Lord. Some of us gave a message, some sang a hymn, some maintained the order, and others distributed tracts and booklets. To be sure, this way brings people to the Lord, and the Lord will honor us in this. We also did this in northern China in 1935. Many nights we went out in groups, and we shouted and sang to bring the people in. Then we would kneel in a circle to surround the people, and some would give a message.

In Taiwan, many saints opened their homes once a week on an evening in which there was no church meeting. They would invite three to eight people and would also invite some brothers and sisters to their homes to help them to give informal testimonies and personal talks. In this way, many people were brought to the Lord. The saints were active in preaching the gospel all the time. Many times we did not have a gospel preaching by the whole church for several months, yet when the announcement was made that the church was going to have baptisms, three hundred people would be baptized. Through what means did these new converts come into the church? It was simply through the personal testimonies.

HELPING THE SAINTS
TO PREACH THE GOSPEL BY MANY MEANS

There are many ways to preach the gospel. The metropolitan centers are crowded with people day by day. There are many "fish," and it is easy to catch one. The only problem is that we may not be prepared to do it, and we may have no intention of doing it. The church must be helped to learn how to pray, how to preach the gospel, and to prepare gospel tracts and good booklets. Then the brothers must have the habit of distributing the booklets, mailing the tracts, and so on, in order to stir up the city and even stir up the country.

More than fifty percent of the people in the United States are at least nominal Christians. Of these, about half are Catholics and half are Protestants, and in addition, many of the nominal Christians are false believers. This still leaves many millions who are unbelievers, Gentiles, to preach the gospel to. Many missionaries are going out from this country to the Philippines and to other countries, but in the United States there are many more millions of unbelievers than in the Philippines. What a big field there is here. I came from the Far East, and I have traveled throughout many nations. I have to say, "Praise the Lord for the United States!" because it is the best field for the Lord's work. We have all the conveniences, and it is so easy to preach the gospel.

If we would do it, it is easy to bring people to the Lord. We should help each of the saints to learn how to preach. We cannot go into detail here, but there are many ways. A nurse can preach as a nurse, and a school teacher can preach as a school teacher. This is what we practice in the Far East. Every member there is a preaching member; they preach all the time, nearly day by day, and so many of the saints simply live for the gospel.

If we do this, this will be a protection to us as Christians. In Ephesians 6:15 Paul tells us that the firm foundation of the gospel is our shoes. Shoes protect us from the earth. If we do not have shoes, our feet become dirty and damaged. To protect our feet from being hurt, damaged, and dirty, we need a good pair of shoes. If as a Christian we do not preach the gospel, we are "barefoot." The best way to keep our feet from being dirtied and damaged by the world is to preach the gospel to our friends, neighbors, and schoolmates, telling them something about the Lord Jesus. To preach the gospel in this way helps us to be better Christians. It always reminds us that we are Christians. We are reminded not to do certain things with persons to whom we have preached the gospel. It is simply because we do not testify for the Lord Jesus that we can do certain things with our friends. We should tell all our friends and neighbors, "I am a proper, normal Christian, and I wish to tell you that you need to love the Lord." Try to do this, and see what will come out. Being a testimony to people helps us to be humble, sincere, careful, faithful, and to try our best to love others. This is the best pair of shoes for our Christian feet. Let us pray for this and try to help all the saints who meet together with us to have such a habit.

At a certain point, when the leading ones of the church realize that the church needs to have a gospel campaign, a gospel meeting, they should call the saints together every evening to have a week of prayer meetings to pray specifically in preparation for the gospel preaching. Then, we need at least one or two weeks more to come together to train them how to preach, how to take care of their relatives, how to invite and bring people to the meeting, and how to come to work together in a coordinated way to preach the gospel in coordination. Some can take care of people, some can distribute tracts, and some can do other things. There are many things to do in a move for the gospel. We especially need to train the brothers and sisters to do the work after the gospel meeting of visiting people. Then, after they are baptized and brought into the church as new converts, the church must care for them. If we practice this, it will be easy for the number of the saints to be doubled by the new converts, and there will be the newness and freshness in the fellowship of the church. To have the same brothers coming together week after week on the Lord's Day becomes old, with no freshness or newness. There is the need for new converts, new members, new "cells."

Here I have given only some general ideas. May the Lord help us to practice these things in the church service.

CHAPTER SIX

REALIZING THE BODY LIFE

Scripture Reading: Rom. 12; Gen. 1:26

By the mercy and grace of the Lord we have seen something of life, and we have seen that in order to experience life we need certain real dealings, including dealing with the flesh, the self, the conscience, the world, and the spirit. All these are for the practical experience of life. If we take care of all these dealings, we will attain to a point where we realize the divine life in the church life. We will realize the Body of Christ, not merely in doctrine but in a practical way in our Christian practice and Christian life; that is, we will realize the real practice of the Body of Christ. Therefore, in this chapter we will see something further concerning the Body of Christ. Although this may be a familiar subject or term for many of us, we look to the Lord that we may see something in a very practical way.

THE EXPERIENCE OF THE BODY OF CHRIST

The book of Romans shows us that the final stage, or experience, of the Christian life is the stage, the experience, of the Body of Christ. Romans speaks of justification, release from sin, sanctification, and walking according to the Spirit. After all these, in Romans 12 we eventually realize the Body of Christ in our experience. If we read this chapter carefully, we will realize that Paul the apostle did not write concerning the Body in the way of doctrine. Rather, he wrote something about the Body of Christ in a very practical way.

Presenting Our Bodies

First, he shows us that if we are going to realize the

experience of the Body of Christ, we must offer ourselves to the Lord. When the apostle came to the matter of this offering, this consecration, he spoke in a very practical way, saying that we need to present our bodies (v. 1). To speak concerning the body is practical. To come to a meeting, for example, we must come in our physical body. To say that we are coming only in our mind or even in our spirit is something "in the air." We may say, "I offer myself to the Lord," but have we offered our body to the Lord? To offer ourselves in a way that is without our body is an offering or a consecration to the Lord "in the air." We can only be in our body; we cannot be "in the air." If we come to a brother or to his home, we must come in the body. If we do not come in the body, the brother will not know how to contact us. Similarly, if we offer ourselves without our body, the Lord will not be able to contact us on the earth. If our offering involves our body, it is practical. We need to offer our body to the Lord.

Not Being Fashioned according to This Age

Second, Paul says, "Do not be fashioned according to this age" (v. 2a). The King James Version uses the word *world* in this verse, but the Greek word means "age," the present part of the world, the part which is before us. The present part of the world is the age. Within the world as a whole there are many ages, age after age. Strictly speaking, we cannot contact the world without contacting the age of the world. We can compare this with being in the United States. We cannot be in this country without being in one of the states. To be in the country, we must be in a state. To not be conformed to the age, the present world, is also something very practical.

Being Transformed by the Renewing of the Mind

Third, we must be transformed by the renewing of the mind (v. 2b). This is something more practical; it is subjectively practical. We need to check how much we as Christians, reborn ones, children of God, have been transformed. We were born as the old creation, so everything within us is old. The mind is old, the will is old, the emotions are old, and the heart and every part of our being are old. Now, we have been regenerated and renewed in the spirit, but how much have we been transformed, renewed, in all the inward parts of our whole being? This is something very subjective and practical; it is not a mere doctrine. Merely listening to and agreeing with this does not work. We must realize that this is practical, something we must experience; otherwise, we do not have it.

Knowing What the Best Will of God Is

We must offer ourselves in the body to the Lord, we must not be conformed to this present age, and we must be transformed by the renewing of our mind. Fourth, we have to discern, know, and test what the best will of God is (v. 2c). If we have all these practical matters, we will then attain to the point where we are able to realize the Body life, the life of the Body of Christ. We may talk about the church life, the Body life, and the Body of Christ, but the realization of the life of the Body of Christ depends on the above four practical matters, three positive and one negative. If we have the practical experiences of offering ourselves in our body to the Lord, of not being conformed to the present age, of being transformed in our old nature, and of having the discernment of the best will of God, we will have the ground to realize the Body life. At this point, we will realize that as people who are regenerated and transformed by the Holy Spirit, we are members of the Body, and as members, what we must experience is something not of this world or of ourselves but something absolutely of Christ Himself. It is at this point that we will know what it means to say, "It is no longer I who live, but it is Christ who lives in me" (Gal. 2:20) and, "For to me, to live is Christ" (Phil. 1:21). We will realize what it means to live not by our self but by Christ as our life, not in the way of doctrine but in the way of life and practical experience.

Today there is the urgent need of this teaching concerning the Body life, but we must realize that the teaching is not for the teaching; it is for life, for the church, for Christ. If the teaching is for its own sake, it will not work. What good is it to have the teaching only for the teaching's sake? All the teaching must be for the church and for Christ. We can have the Body life in no way other than to consecrate ourselves in a practical way, to offer ourselves as a practical people in the body, not as a people "in the air." Moreover, we must not conform ourselves to this present age. We must be separated, sanctified, and different from this age as a particular people, and we must be transformed. Then we will realize the Body of Christ as a life that is absolutely not independent, individual, and not of the natural self, but a life which is Christ Himself to be experienced by us in a corporate way.

THE BODY AS THE ULTIMATE INTENTION, GOAL, AND DESIRE OF GOD'S HEART

This Body is the ultimate intention, goal, and desire of God's heart. What God is seeking in this universe is simply this Body. In Genesis 1, God had two intentions in His creation of man. One is to express Himself, and the other is to deal with His enemy. God created man in His own image for the purpose that man may express God. In this creation, God committed His authority to man to deal with the enemy. The image is for the expression, and the authority is to deal with the enemy of God. These are the two intentions in God's creation of man, one on the positive side and the other on the negative side. Both the positive side and the negative side of God's intention are a matter of a corporate Body. To express God in Christ through the Holy Spirit, strictly speaking, is not a matter of individuals but a matter of a corporate Body.

More than thirty years ago I received the knowledge that God is seeking a Body, but I did not know how to realize and explain this. It seemed that there were no human words to express, define, or explain such a divine matter, but I gradually realized more concerning the Body. We are all persons with a body. As such, we are all a very good figure or type. As persons we need to be expressed. Can our person be expressed by separate, individual members? It is true that we have ears, a nose, lips, eyes, and fingers; we have many members, but they cannot express us in a separate, individual way. We cannot cut off our ears or nose and present them as our expression. Our person must be expressed by our whole body in a corporate way. The whole body is needed to express a person. We are not bodies; we are members of the one Body.

In the whole universe Christ has only one Body, and it is through this one Body that He is expressed. God in Christ through the Holy Spirit is expressed in the one Body.

God needs a Body, not merely many members. Why is the church so weak among many Christians? Why do we sense weakness, confusion, many negative things, and things other than Christ Himself in every kind of Christian group? It is because they are like a body whose members have been separated and scattered in an individual way. We cannot see a person but only separated and scattered members. To have separated and scattered members is an awful condition which causes many troubles and things which need to be cleared up. This is the real situation of Christians today. We may meet group after group of Christians, but they are separated and scattered members. When we come among them, we do not sense the reality of the Body. We do not sense that there is a Body which always expresses Christ. Rather, we can only realize separated and scattered members. Moreover, even though the members are separated and scattered, they are still able to fight one another. It is as if they are good for nothing but fighting, not with the enemy of God but with one another. This is simply because there is no realization of the Body life.

THE PRACTICAL STEPS TO REALIZING THE BODY LIFE

Giving Up the Self

Let us consider the practical steps to realizing the Body life. If we are going to practice and realize the Body life, we first must give up our self. The word *self* is a small word, but it is a practical issue. In order to realize the Body life, we must always remember to give up our self, self-seeking, self-centeredness, self-opinion, self-intention, and self-exaltation. If we bring in even a small amount of self, we bring a cancer into the Body. There is no need for us to do anything more serious; to bring in only a small amount of self is enough for the enemy to damage the Body. This is why we have said that the first item of the spiritual "charter" of the church is the cross. The cross must check our self.

I do know what I am saying. What I am speaking is not a lecture; rather, I am pointing out the practical steps to realizing the Body. If we intend to practice the real Body life, we must be one hundred percent careful concerning the self. The first thing which damages the Body life so much is the self. The things of the self are the little foxes which ruin the vineyards when they are in blossom (S. S. 2:15). We may say, "I have not done anything wrong. My intention toward the church is good." This may be true, but a little thing within us—the self—damages the Body. It is not necessary to have a big thing to damage the Body; even a little thing damages it. A small mote can damage the eye, and when the eye is damaged, the whole body cannot work. It is the same with the self.

Losing Our Independence

Second, we must lose our independence. To practice the church life we must learn never to be independent. There is no independence in the Body life; there is only dependence. None of the members of our body can be independent. Independence simply means death for the Body and death for the members. We should look at this matter not doctrinally but very practically. This is a vital matter, a matter of life and death. For a hand to declare independence means death for it.

You may say that you are not independent, that you are a dependent member of the Body. However, I wish to ask in a practical rather than doctrinal way: To whom are you related? If we ask a finger, it will say it is related to the hand and to the other fingers, and if we ask the hand, it will say it is related to the arm. These members can point out to whom they are related. However, one may be a good brother with everyone's acclaim, but he may not be able to point out to whom he is related. He is good to every brother and sister, but he is independent of everyone and related to no one.

It is wrong to form a party with someone because we have the same opinion. This is sectarian, and it causes division upon division. However, in the church we must be related to someone. This proves we are not independent. To be related to a few saints without forming a party is a hard lesson to learn. It is easy to not be related, and it is even easier to be related with others to form a party. Two brothers may often come together, and it may seem that they are of one mind and can easily pray together. If one says, "Hallelujah," the other says, "Amen," and if the other says, "Hallelujah," the first one says, "Praise the Lord!" They may seem to be of one mind, but this may not be the proper relatedness. Rather, it may be a party, a sect, a division with a sectarian spirit. This is wrong.

Still, as members in the church we must be related to someone or ones. All the brothers and sisters must be related one with another. If we say that we are practicing the church life, we must lose and give up our independence. The independent living must be one hundred percent given up.

Try to check yourself as to whom you are related. If you check with me, I would say that I am related with many saints locally and even more universally. On the negative side, if any of them would express even a little that they do not agree with what I am doing, I would stop right away and go along with them. On the positive side, what I do is confirmed and sealed by them. They are one with me in the spirit, and they may say, "Okay, brother, go ahead; we are with you one hundred percent." Here is a real, practical, and serious lesson for us to learn. Without this, there is no possibility to realize the Body life. If we still have our independence, we may be very nice to one another, but we can never realize the Body life among us.

Keeping the Harmony

Third, if we are going to realize the Body life, we must seriously and heartily learn always to keep the harmony. This does not mean that in doing something wrong we are in harmony to be wrong, and it does not mean that we never have disagreements or discussions. We may even have arguments, but we must argue in harmony. It is possible to argue in harmony. Many brothers and sisters have a beautiful marriage life of arguing in harmony. A couple may invite someone to their home for a love feast and fellowship. The brother may want to serve Cantonese food, but the sister may want to prepare American food. In this way they may argue, but they still argue in harmony, happiness, and joy. This is a beautiful life and a beautiful argument. When someone comes to their home, he can sense the beauty and see how beautifully the couple argues in harmony. Of course, we must learn the lesson to be careful in arguments. Many times it is easy to be in the flesh and in the self in arguments. Yet we can still discuss many things and even argue many things for the Lord's sake and for His testimony, interest, kingdom, and Body, but we argue in harmony. If we can keep the harmony, we can continue to argue, but if we cannot keep the harmony, we must stop the argument. Learn the lessons of keeping the harmony.

Harmony is the real expression of the oneness among the Lord's children. There is a difference between oneness and harmony. We may say that we are one, and we may even be one, but we may not have harmony. All the parts of a piano are one, but when we play the piano, it may not have harmony. A piano must be tuned to have harmony. We may have oneness without harmony, but to be sure, if we have harmony, we have oneness because harmony is something more than oneness. The real expression of the oneness of the Body is harmony.

I have seen the beautiful harmony. When we have harmony in the church, we realize the Lord's presence very much, and we automatically and spontaneously realize all His riches for the church. There is no need to ask for and seek the spiritual things such as spiritual infilling, outpouring, and gifts. If we simply have the harmony, all these things will come. I know what I am speaking about because I have seen this. Learn the lesson to keep the harmony.

Harmony is a very tender and deep matter. It controls and regulates us very much. If we truly have a sincere heart to keep the harmony among the Lord's children, we will be very regulated and ruled by the heavenly reality. We will be governed, controlled, and directed by the inner life, the inner anointing, and the inner presence of the Lord. We will be controlled in acting, speaking, and even thinking, and we will be very fine in many matters. We will be very tender in order to keep the harmony. Then we can argue with one another, yet in a very tender and fine way and very much in harmony.

Remembering That All Things Are Secondary to Christ and His Body

Fourth, we must always keep in mind that nothing is more important than the Lord Christ Himself and His Body. Always remember that all things are secondary; only the Lord Himself and His Body are primary. All things are not for themselves but for the Lord Christ and for His Body, the church. Sometimes we may do or speak something and make it more important than Christ and the church. However, all things, even teachings, doctrines, truths, and experiences, are for the church and for the Head, the Lord. We should not do anything or insist on anything in a way of damaging the church life even a little.

When I speak of the kingdom truths or other truths, I have no intention to force anyone to believe what I believe or to take the same way I take. That is absolutely not my intention. My intention is that these truths will help others to love the Lord, seek Him more, realize the proper spiritual life, and practice the church life more and more. As long as one loves the Lord, seeks Him, experiences Him, lives by Him, and comes together with the saints to exalt and exhibit Him more and more, I am happy. I will be happy even if someone fully differs from me in certain truths. We do not have the truths for their own sake; rather, they are all for Christ and the church.

On the other hand, if someone receives these truths and agrees with them, he must not argue with others or try to convince them. We are not preaching truths; we are preaching Christ. Our intention, commission, and burden is not to preach doctrines but to preach Christ and minister Him to others. Of course, sometimes we need doctrines and truths as the means to help people to know Christ more, but the truths are not for the truths; the truths must be for Christ, the church, and the proper spiritual life. As long as people receive Christ, experience Christ, and love the Lord more and more, we are happy and praise the Lord, regardless of the truths concerning the kingdom, the rapture, or other matters. We do not care for those matters; we care for the Lord Himself and

His Body. Do not go to preach these truths and argue with people about them. If we do this, we have completely failed the Lord. We must realize that the aim, the goal, is Christ and the church, the Lord and His Body.

We must keep the above four matters. We need to reject our self, give up our independence, always do the best to keep the harmony, and always keep in mind that nothing is as important as Christ and His church. When we do this, we are in the reality of the Body life. I simply present this to you in a brief way with few words. Let us try to learn these lessons. Then we will realize how practical they are, yet how much of a test they are. These are testing lessons, lessons that always test and check us. The self, the independence, the disharmony, and the overemphasis of matters other than Christ and His church damage and kill the church life.

Let us learn the lessons along this line and toward this goal. Learn the lessons to give up our self, to forget our independence, and to keep the sweet, fine, and tender harmony among the saints. Moreover, always remember that we are here for nothing but our dear Lord and His Body; this is our commission, our business. If we do this, I am assured that in a very short time we will all be in the reality of the Body life. Then there will be the real building up of the church. We can be assured that all the riches of Christ for His church will be with us and will be realized by us, and we will see a wonderful and beautiful situation. There is no need for us to seek other spiritual things. We simply need to go along with the Lord in these lessons.